KU-125-056

Contents

History Data Service

Digitising History
A Guide to Creating Digital Resources from Historical Documents

Sean Townsend
Cressida Chappell
Oscar Struijvé

Produced by Oxbow Books for the Arts and Humanities Data Service

ISBN 1 900188 91 0
ISSN 1463-5194

© Sean Townsend, Cressida Chappell and Oscar Struijvé 1999

Cover Illustration © Sophie Chambers

The right of Sean Townsend, Cressida Chappell and Oscar Struijvé to be identified as the Authors of this Work has been asserted by them in accordance with the Copyright, Designs and Patents Act 1988.

All material supplied via the Arts and Humanities Data Service is protected by copyright, and duplication or sale of all or part of any of it is not permitted, except as otherwise permitted under the Copyright, Designs and Patents Act 1988. Permission for any other use must be obtained from the Arts and Humanities Data Service.

This book is available direct from

Oxbow Books, Park End Place, Oxford OX1 1HN
(Phone: 01865–241249; Fax: 01865–794449)

and

The David Brown Book Company
PO Box 511, Oakville, CT 06779, USA
(Phone: 860–945–9329; Fax: 860–945–9468)

or from our website
www.oxbowbooks.com

Printed in Great Britain at
The Short Run Press
Exeter

Acknowledgements

We would like to express our sincere thanks to the following people who reviewed this guide, offered suggestions for its improvement, and contributed to its shape.

Birgit Austin, History Data Service

Christina Bashford, Oxford Brookes University

Hamish James, History Data Service

Val Kinsler, 100% Proof

Roger Middleton, University of Bristol

Jon Press, Bath Spa University College

Lorna Scammell, University of Newcastle

Astrid Wissenburg, Kings College London

Chapter 1: Introduction

1.1 BACKGROUND

This guide has been commissioned by the History Data Service (HDS) as part of the Arts and Humanities Data Service (AHDS) publication series *Guides to Good Practice in the Creation and Use of Digital Resources*. The series aims to provide guidance about applying recognised good practice and standards to the creation and use of digital resources in the arts and humanities.

The HDS is funded by the Joint Information Systems Committee (JISC) of the UK Higher Education Funding Councils to collect, catalogue, manage, preserve and encourage the re-use of historical digital resources. The HDS is located in the social science Data Archive at the University of Essex and is the AHDS service provider for the historical disciplines. The AHDS offers services to the archaeology, history, performing arts, textual studies and visual arts communities. It consists of five subject-based Service Providers (Archaeology Data Service, History Data Service, Performing Arts Data Service, Oxford Text Archive and Visual Arts Data Service) and a managing Executive.

1.2 AIMS AND OBJECTIVES

This guide is intended as a reference work for individuals and organisations involved with, or planning, the computerisation of historical source documents. It aims to recommend good practice and standards that are generic and relevant to a range of data creation situations, from student projects through to large-scale research projects. The guide focuses on the creation of tabular data suitable for use in databases, spreadsheets or statistics packages, however, many of the guidelines are more widely applicable. For other approaches to the computerisation of historical source documents see Woollard and Denley 1996; Feldman 1995; Gahan and Hannibal 1997; Kelle 1995; Miles and Huberman 1994; Robinson 1993; and Robinson 1994.

The time and resources invested in the creation of digital resources can easily be placed in jeopardy because hardware and software become obsolete, and magnetic media degrade. Long-term preservation is essential if this investment is to be safeguarded. Digital resources need to be preserved and migrated through changing technologies in order that they will continue to be accessible in the future. However, the extent to which a digital resource can be preserved without significant information loss is largely dependent on decisions taken during the data creation process; this guide seeks to explain how to ensure that a digital resource is suitable for preservation and migration.

Many historical digital resources potentially have significant and long-term value to the research and teaching community. The time and resources invested in their creation can only be fully realised if they are suitable for re-use both by the data creator and by others. Such suitability, however, is again largely dependent on decisions taken during the data creation process; this guide also aims to offer advice about creating digital resources which are suitable for re-use and which will be of long-term value to the research and teaching community.

1.3 OUTLINE

The guide is divided into eight chapters. Chapter 2 offers guidance about effectively designing and managing a data creation project. Chapter 3 focuses on the process of transferring historical source documents into digital form and designing a database to hold the digital information; it also encourages data creators to think carefully about the relationship between the sources and the database. Chapter 4 takes a more technical focus and concentrates on the question of data formats and preservation, explaining how to ensure that a digital resource can be preserved without significant information loss. Chapter 5 stresses the importance of thoroughly documenting a data creation project, and describes the elements essential to good documentation. Chapter 6 describes the benefits of archiving data and includes a guide to depositing data with the HDS. Chapter 7 contains a glossary of terms and a bibliography of recommended further reading.

Chapter 2 :
Managing Digital Resource Creation Projects

2.1 INTRODUCTION

What justifies yet another introduction to project management? A wealth of literature already describes every imaginable aspect of management, project-related or not. Why re-invent the wheel?

The answer is simple: this chapter does not attempt to re-iterate existing literature on project management. Rather it intends to:

- Make existing literature and good practice accessible.
- Link some key management issues, concepts and practice to the specific topic of this guide – the creation of digital resources from historical documents.
- Do so whilst emphasising the value and importance of flexibility and, in particular, re-usability of digital resources, within and beyond the scope of a project.

In the context of this guide, good project management does not necessarily imply *more* management, or the use of *formal methods and techniques*. The number of people involved in a project, their level of experience and the size and complexity of the tasks at hand will influence, among many other factors, what constitutes the right amount and the right level of formalisation. Examples exist of situations where there is plenty of (perceived) management activity, but very little project indeed.

A significant number of projects within the historical disciplines are externally funded. This implies that aims, objectives and project deliverables, as well as the available and required resources and evidence of good project management, have to be made explicit in order to maximise the likelihood of obtaining financial support.

In essence, this chapter states a strong case for carefully planning, organising and monitoring the process of creating a digital resource. These activities will be easier and more successful if they are underpinned by clearly defined aims, objectives and deliverables, and an analysis of opportunities and risks.

This chapter will *not* describe specific techniques and tools or formal, structured, methodologies for project management. Day (1995) provides a pragmatic introduction to project management with many examples, using a widely available tool, Microsoft Project®, to illustrate various planning techniques and concepts. Slightly more daunting, and detailed, but certainly useful for more complex projects is the formal method PRINCE, a 'structured method for effective project management', fully described in CCTA (1997). More closely related to the specific scope of this guide is Harvey and Press (1996), dealing with the subject of databases and research methods aimed at the historical community. In particular chapter 4

(Harvey and Press 1996, 73–97) provides information related to management of resource creation projects. Howard and Sharp (1994) give guidance on project management for those embarking on digital resource creation within the context of a student research project, on all levels up to PhD. Student projects are special in that they often have limited staffing (typically one researcher: the student), limited resources and very tight deadlines. Non-student projects with similar characteristics may also benefit from some of the recommendations in Howard and Sharp (1994, 46–66 and 121–47).

2.2 THE CONTEXT OF DIGITAL RESOURCE CREATION

The creation of digital resources from historical documents as a self-contained project with a separate budget and resources is still unusual (see Section 3.2). It is often undertaken as part of, or in support of, a programme of research. This chapter concentrates on this typical scenario, but many of the issues and recommendations also apply in different contexts, like the creation or improvement of teaching resources. Alternatively, the creation of digital resources 'simply happens' as a by-product of research, teaching, archiving or other activities. From a management point of view this 'by-product' scenario is not ideal, as it implies that the digital resource is not a deliverable and is potentially created or treated with less care. It is, however, entirely possible that during such a project a significant digital resource can be (or has been) created, which was not anticipated. This can be treated as an opportunity to enrich and enhance the outcomes of the project. Consequently, an attempt should be made to adjust the project plan and – if required – to re-allocate resources in order to see creation and documentation of the digital resource through to completion, and to do so according to good practice (see Chapter 3, Chapter 4 and Chapter 5). If this is successful, the project can continue as intended, but with resource creation now an explicit component of the project plan (see Section 2.4).

2.3 PLANNING DIGITAL RESOURCE CREATION

Most publications about project management put considerable emphasis on planning aspects. It is important to emphasise that planning does not stop when projects start or receive funding, but is a continuing activity. It makes perfect sense to allocate time throughout the life span of the project to revisit the project plan and, if appropriate, to adjust it as part of monitoring progress. Projects do not under-perform because they adjust or re-focus their objectives, but because they neglect to do so in changing environments and circumstances. Responsibilities and authority related to planning activities (including changes to priorities, specifications and timetable, or requests for these) must be clearly defined. They should be communicated to and understood by the whole project team, including researchers, support staff and project managers.

In situations where project management is not approached in a formal way, benefits can still be obtained from careful planning, organisation and monitoring of resources and progress. This allows appropriate intervention if progress towards aims is not as planned, new opportunities arise or the cost of achieving progress exceeds the original allocations in terms of time, budget, or resources. Fundamental to good management is the attempt to understand at an early stage the potential risks to successful completion (on time, within budget and according to plan or specification). This makes it much easier to anticipate adverse situations in the various stages of digital resource creation projects, and to manage the risks involved. Within the context of this guide, it is important to note that the use of information technology, essential to digital resource creation, is often considered a major contributor to project risks, in particular if the technologies on which the project depends are new or unfamiliar to the project team.

Project planning goes beyond planning the contents and structure of the digital resource and the accompanying documentation. It includes allocating available resources (computers, software, office space, staff etc.) to the various interdependent activities, which together constitute a project, and scheduling these activities. In order to do this effectively, projects are often divided into 'manageable' phases or stages, which in turn can be broken down into tasks or activities. The allocation of resources can be done on the level of individual activities. It is considered good practice to do this in such a way that dependencies between activities are minimised, where possible. The main advantage of this approach is that problems and delays in some tasks will only affect a limited number of other tasks, on the basis of known dependencies. Making dependencies explicit, helps to identify the critical path, encompassing those activities for which delays will result in delayed completion of the project. It also facilitates parallel execution of tasks, and makes it easier to distribute responsibility between members of a project team. Many techniques and visualisation and analysis tools exist to assist in these and other aspects of project planning. Some of them are briefly introduced in Harvey and Press (1996, 75–80) and Day (1995, 11–28).

2.4 CREATING BREATHING SPACE: SPECIFICATIONS AND PRIORITIES

The strong links often found between resource creation and research, impact on planning. If resource creation is undertaken as part of a wider project, it will have to be planned and scheduled in conjunction with other activities, many of which will depend on or affect successful creation of the digital resource. For this reason, key resource creation activities more often than not tend to become part of a project's critical path (see Day 1995, 25–26). In order to minimise the likelihood of delays in these activities, which would affect the entire project, a distinction can be introduced between a *minimum specification* of the digital resource and its documentation and a *full specification*. The minimum specification includes essential requirements only; the full specification includes optional characteristics. By planning on the basis of the full specification, it becomes possible to 'fall back' upon a minimum specification when necessary. This approach reduces or even eliminates delays without having to make ad hoc decisions. This is one way of introducing slack or reducing the critical path. It shows how planning makes it possible to anticipate and accommodate circumstances which potentially endanger the progress of a project.

By effectively *prioritising* the scope and characteristics of the digital resource and documentation, resource creation projects become more flexible and effective in dealing with potential delays. The criteria for regarding elements of the digital resource and documentation as either essential or optional need to be chosen with much care, and should take into account how omission of particular resource or documentation elements will affect (re)usability. Section 3.2 will discuss this topic in more detail.

2.5 THE LINK BETWEEN RESOURCE CREATION AND RESEARCH

As mentioned earlier in this chapter, digital resource creation is often closely related to a specific research agenda. This has a number of implications, both desirable and undesirable, which can be treated as *opportunities* and *risks*.

Opportunities include:

- If carefully managed, a research agenda can act as a testbed environment for usability of a digital resource, beyond the scope of the original ('minimum') set of questions a project intends to answer. The separation between resource and project objectives advocated in Section 3.2.2 is crucial for capitalising on this opportunity.
- Resource creation, undertaken as a stand-alone project, can easily become over-ambitious in scope. A close link with a research project or teaching purpose provides a specific focus for digital resources and helps to define their boundaries. This safeguards against over-ambitious aims and objectives.
- 'Creating digital resources' is often difficult to justify as a purpose in itself. Linking digital resource creation to research activities may increase the potential for acquiring external funding. Many important resource creation activities would never have been funded separately.

The link between resource creation activities and research also introduces risks. These include:

- *Digital resource creation is often considered secondary to the research*, and only receives attention in direct relation to specific research objectives. It can become tempting to transcribe historical sources only partially, or to structure digital resources in ways considered suitable or ideal for the specific research agenda. Existing standards may be ignored or only receive limited attention. As a result, the resource may lack the flexibility to contribute to answering questions other than the original ones. This is in many respects the flip side of the first two opportunities mentioned above.
- *The time, effort, skills and money involved in resource creation are often under-estimated.* Data analysis and software development can be time-consuming and require specific skills. Suitable hard- and software can be expensive. An emphasis on research can result in late recognition of these facts, if they are recognised at all. Because digital resource creation is likely to underpin the wider research agenda, this can be a serious risk for the intended research.
- *Accurate and complete documentation may not be given high priority*, because the focus is on use of the digital resource within the research project, where it is often assumed that everyone is familiar with the specifics of its creation and structure, or has easy access to expert knowledge. Section 2.6 of this guide explains why complete and accurate project documentation is important, and Chapter 5 provides a detailed overview of data documentation issues.

An additional risk, not specifically related to resource creation within the context of research projects, involves copyright and intellectual property right issues. Increasingly, projects involving digital resource creation encounter problems to do with these issues. It is important that potential issues of rights management and clearance are recognised early on and adequate expertise and funding is found, if warranted by the nature of the situation.

The lists of opportunities and risks in this section are far from complete, and are only meant to indicate some important issues for consideration when creating digital resources. It is good practice to list as many opportunities and risks as possible before a project starts. By identifying suitable courses of action for different scenarios, the project becomes more robust. In particular, *anticipating risks* can significantly reduce the number and impact of unpleasant surprises during a project.

2.6 DOCUMENTING THE PROJECT

Documentation, or rather documenting, is an important aspect of project management for more than one reason. First of all, accurate and complete documentation is a corner stone of project management. It is the basic mechanism that allows the ability to plan ahead, monitor and evaluate progress and to take action where appropriate. Secondly, documenting the project equals documenting the process. If one of the aims of the project is to transform information contained in historical documents into digital resources, it becomes impossible to establish the relation between these resources and the historical documents without documentation of the transformation process and the often-complex decisions taken during this process. In other words, the provenance of a digital resource delivered by a project may be lost without accurate documentation of the project itself. A third reason for producing complete yet concise project documentation is the need to ensure maximum continuity and minimise disruption when faced with changes in the composition of the project team.

2.7 MANAGING REAL WORLD PROJECTS: TOUGH DECISIONS

Most real world projects adopt some measure of 'systematic' management, ranging from largely informal approaches to extensive use of formal methods and techniques. In most cases this will help to complete the project with at least a subset of its original aims and objectives achieved. However, even adhering to every applicable standard, guideline and 'good practice', and understanding and applying suitable techniques does not completely safeguard against the impact of unanticipated, adverse, situations. Funding cuts, staff changes and illness, are just a few examples of problems which may force projects to drop deliverables or lower 'minimum' standards. The question that must then be answered is: 'what can be salvaged?' or rather: 'what is worth salvaging?'. There is, unsurprisingly, no set answer, but the concept of re-usability mentioned in Section 2.1, provides at least a basis for establishing criteria for decisions of this kind. In other words: trying to maximise the amount of *properly documented, re-usable data* is a sensible point of departure in situations like this.

2.8 SUMMARY

In this chapter an attempt is made to build a bridge between good practice(s) in project management and the specific characteristics and requirements of digital resource creation from historical documents. It emphasises that proper planning and management is essential to achieve project objectives, and is instrumental in successfully attracting funding through a research grant bidding process. It is suggested that the ability to respond successfully to unanticipated, adverse influences can be increased significantly, by distinguishing between required and optional characteristics of a digital resource. The typical scenario of digital resource creation within the context of research activities, and how this creates specific opportunities and risks, is discussed. Maximising the re-usability of resources and documentation is recommended as a lead principle in digital resource creation from historical documents. This benefits both the project and future research, and cannot be achieved without proper and complete documentation of the whole process.

This chapter is generic in nature. The following chapters will present more specific and detailed guidelines and will cement the basic structure introduced here.

Chapter 3 : From Source to Database

3.1 INTRODUCTION

It hardly needs saying that the act of creating a digital historical database involves the process of converting information from one format (paper) to another (digital). This conversion process is ultimately the essence of creating the resource, and those embarking on the endeavour need to think very hard about exactly what it is they are about to do. Talking to others who have gone through similar processes in related disciplines, reading appropriate literature, and evaluating and using a range of database technologies are possible initial starting points. The much-used maxim 'Garbage In – Garbage Out' is, unsurprisingly, appropriate here as the decisions taken and methodology employed in this critical stage of the resource's development, define the future value and usefulness of the resource. Bad judgements and fudged decisions at the design stage are almost always amplified in the final product which, at best, can make the database extremely problematic to use and, at worst, completely worthless.

In most cases, creating a historical database that has real benefit to the scholarly community is not particularly difficult. Ultimately what is required from the creator is a sound design, the application of absolute consistency and comprehensive documentation. In fact, consistency and documentation will be over-riding themes in this guide – they are extremely important. Creators should think about the database design as a conceptual framework that outlines the process of conversion from paper to digital. The design stage dictates in what way and in which forms the digital version *represents* the original paper source. This chapter therefore intends to guide creators through some of the issues involved in this conversion process, to ensure that their creation benefits both them and potential users to the maximum possible extent. Needless to say, what are presented in this chapter are not hard-and-fast rules, but rather guidelines which creators are encouraged to adopt, adjusting them for their own needs and situation.

3.2 DEFINING AIMS AND OBJECTIVES OF THE PROJECT

Anyone involved in a project (or potential project) that involves the creation of a digital resource has to think in terms of a finished product. Given that few projects in the UK are funded solely on the basis of resource creation, those involved in the project have to balance the requirements of providing academic research results with the need to produce a database that is both of value to them and potentially to others. It is this balancing act, and the implications it has for the resultant data, that this section discusses.

3.2.1 General project objectives

All historical research of this kind involves the subtle synthesis of traditional research approaches with computer-based methodologies. Ultimately, the computer is a research tool and is used to explore themes, issues or important questions. Perhaps the best diagrammatic summary can be found in Harvey and Press (1996, 3). Traditionally the focus of most historical research projects has been the publication of findings. The gathering, management and analysis of documentary evidence is part of the necessary process of historical discourse, but usually the source material does not have a tangible place in the final objective of a project. Unless the work involves a scholarly edition of some kind, the sources are relegated to the background whilst the research findings take centre stage. Funding is provided for historians on the basis that new insights into the field are produced, rather than the publication of existing historical documents. Coping with the pressure to produce results is at the heart of all research programmes.

However, for those whose project envisages the creation of digital data, this traditional model of practice soon becomes of limited use. This guide strongly encourages researchers in this field to consider carefully their 'general project objectives' in this case. In other words, researchers working on historical projects that include resource creation should think about their sources, the questions to be asked, the database design phase, the database creation phase and the database documentation phase. Some of these may not be linear stages (for example documentation is best tackled on-the-fly: see Chapter 5), yet careful planning and preparation will be essential to the project's success. For an excellent summary commentary, see Harvey and Press (1996, 76–81). It would not be an over-simplification to suggest that the inclusion of database creation genuinely requires an innovative approach to research projects. Yet perhaps 'Is database technology appropriate for my research?' might be the very first question any project team or individual might ask. If it is established that such technology is appropriate, a range of issues and considerations to be tackled emerge. There are a number of ways in which the resource creation element of a project may have an impact on the project as a whole. The following questions need to be considered:

- Are all the elements of the source suitable for transcription to tabular database form? If not, what is the strategy for working with problematic elements?
- Are the research goals of the project feasible, especially given the resource creation element of the project?
- Are enough resources allocated to meet the research and data objectives (time especially)?
- Does the project recognise the wider value of the source material? Would the digital source be of benefit to future researchers?
- Has project planning provided an acceptable balance between resource creation and data analysis?
- Is the project aware of outstanding copyright issues involved when replicating original source documents?

Creators should consider the above as a checklist. Notice that traditional research projects do not have to grapple with such questions.

3.2.2 Data objectives

One of the central issues that historians need to know of any database is 'what questions can be asked of it?' Of course, all databases, whether statistical or textual in character, have a finite analysis compass, all are limited in some way, but lack of forethought can lead to a resource that has an extremely limited potential audience and which, therefore, however technically perfect, will be of only very limited wider use. Take the fictitious example of a project that is exploring nineteenth-century migration patterns from census enumerators books (CEBs). The project team has decided that their database will contain only five fields, namely 'Surname', 'Forename', 'Age', 'Place of Enumeration' and 'Place of Birth'. Although this is a completely legitimate project decision, it is clear that such a resource can only be used to study migration, and therefore has only a niche market, and one in which the project team itself may have already explored the issues in sufficient detail. Given that CEBs contain information that goes beyond merely the study of migration, the project team might consider the option that they could in fact produce a more complete database, transcribing more fields than they need, and so provide wider benefits to the scholarly community in general. Taking this view would almost certainly add extra importance to their project and ensure its citation across historical discourse, despite project-focused limited research objectives. (Consider the Mormon transcription of the entire 1881 Census (GSU and FFHS 1997). Their extracted indices of names and birthplaces are of use only to genealogists. However, their original work which transcribed the entire CEBs has ensured that this project not only has use beyond genealogy, but also happened to create a very important digital historical resource.)

The point is that resource creators should carefully consider the extent to which they can separate the database resource itself from the project objectives. Creators should recognise at an early stage the value of their original source documents in a wider sense. Thus, if the resources exist, creators should design the database not solely on the variables they are themselves interested in, but should consider conversion of the material as a whole. Traditionally, the creation of research databases has been solely driven by the need to extract results within the project time frame. As a consequence, a whole swathe of digital databases have been created (and archived) that cannot be used to answer questions beyond those the original researchers were asking. If more valuable resources are to exist, then projects need to factor in the necessary requirements for considering their database as a 'structured edition' of the original source in as much as this is feasible. This, in a sense, is a different slant to the seemingly 'all or nothing' approach of the old 'Source Oriented vs. Model Oriented' argument (Denley 1994) as it is something of a compromise between the two.

The 'data objectives' of any project of this nature need to be considered carefully. All too often the data materials are left as the afterthought of a project, which are offered for deposit with a data archive out of obligation rather than in a genuine attempt to provide a new and interesting resource. Yet many data collections held by the HDS are thoroughly commendable. What distinguishes these key resources is that the creators have planned carefully and given the creation and maintenance of their database a high level of priority. These are projects that have precisely defined their data-related objectives and have employed significant resources in ensuring that such objectives are met. It is also extremely important to note that the capacity to create a valuable and meaningful resource need not impinge on the project's ability to produce satisfactory academic results. Indeed, it can provide significant academic benefits for the original researcher/s in the ability to reflect on research and re-visit their complete database over time.

As a data-focused good practice checklist, consider the following:

- Is the project aware of its data needs?
- Has the project a clear idea of intended data volume?
- Are the resources set-aside for data entry, validation, management and documentation sufficient?
- Is there a disaster recovery strategy at the outset (e.g. data back-ups)?
- Does the project, overall, have sufficient technical expertise at hand?
- Has the project settled on and tested the target software application?

All of the above points are pure common sense. For smaller, one-person based, projects some of the above may of course not be applicable. Yet even for the smallest data gathering endeavour, issues of data back-up and careful technical planning remain important considerations. The over-riding guideline here is to consider the possible wider interest of the source material, and also to ensure that the new digital database is of high quality and usability. Achieving this may require extra planning, but the end result would reflect on those involved very highly indeed. The purpose of defining aims and objectives carefully is that it allows those involved in the project to plan ahead and to base research around database creation.

3.3 LINKS BETWEEN SOURCE AND DATABASE

It is probably worth stating right at the outset that a database is not a historical source. A computer cannot represent all of the characteristics of an original document and even high-resolution digital images (currently the best copy of an original source in digital form) (Jaritz 1991) do not convey every nuance of the original (paper type, condition, size, smell, texture etc.). As this guide is primarily concerned with character-based database systems, the shortcomings of the database version relative to the original can immediately be recognised.

In reality, the shortcomings of a properly designed database to a historian are not profound. Historians have always filtered the crucial elements of information and it is relatively irrelevant in what format these data are made available. Although the Post-modernist critics of history would probably shriek at the very notion of a further subjective representation of an original highly subjective document (Evans 1997), it is important to recognise that a well-designed and implemented database can be one of the most powerful tools for historical enquiry. The key is establishing exactly how the database represents the original, maintaining clarity and avoiding ambiguity in both explanation and implementation of this often-complex relationship. This section of the guide will provide some suggestions on how this can be achieved, and hence immeasurably increase the value of the digital resource.

3.3.1 Source assessment

Knowing as much about the source as possible is a prime requisite for a successful resource creation project. Apart from anything else, it is an exercise in problem anticipation. For some interesting real world examples of this, see Harvey and Press 1991; Green 1989 and Millet 1987. It is something of a truism to say that some source types transfer to tabular form rather better than others do. One problem that historians creating tabular databases have recounted on numerous occasions is the difficulty in making a real world source document 'fit' into the rigid artificial model of the desktop data analysis package. Other analysis systems that can deal with textual non-structured data are available, and many historians have used such tools in the face of the restrictions of purely tabular databases. For examples where researchers have abandoned the formal relational or tabular database approach, see Denley and Woollard 1995.

Many projects deal with multiple rather than single sources. Resource creators are advised to consider each particular source on its own merits and evaluate the material's viability or otherwise for digital transference. This could be considered a selection process by which certain materials can be deemed suitable for transcription into database form, whereas creators may deem that other materials present too many difficulties and would not form part of a database. One of the key dangers to avoid is the situation where the project wastes resources on a difficult source because it was not identified as a potential problem at the outset.

Historical sources in the real world unfortunately do not always fit neatly into the 'good for tables' or 'bad for tables' categories. Very often a source will *in general* be suitable for the creation of a highly structured database but will include elements, possibly significant elements, which are not so suitable. If material is deemed to be suitable for a structured database in general but with a small proportion of problematic elements, then the project needs to think carefully about how these difficult aspects can be dealt with effectively. One possible approach is to digitise these elements in full but leave them outside of the core database application. For an example of how a project has tackled this problem effectively, see Hatton *et al.* (1997). Provided the main body of the source forms the basis of a viable core database, then creators should not become obsessed with the incorporation of every microelement within it. More often than not, this will simply be impossible anyway. Documenting this filtering process is, however, an extremely valuable and worthwhile process.

3.3.2 Will the source 'fit'?

Modern desktop database applications are extremely sophisticated pieces of software. However, despite this sophistication, all relational database systems essentially operate on an identical data model. Some systems have extended or altered the functionality of this model, but the core model has remained unchanged for almost twenty years (Date 1993; Harvey and Press 1996, 102–39). The relational model is based on the premise that the database is formed of related tables whose composition takes the form of rows as individual items and columns as fields of information about those items. This rectangular structure was designed primarily for use in the transaction-based business world, and so its application to real (particularly historical) documents can have a number of significant shortcomings. For the most convincing and consistent attack on the relational model for use with historical sources see the articles of Manfred Thaller (Thaller 1980; Thaller 1988a; Thaller 1988b; Thaller 1989 and Thaller 1991). It is also important to assess the response to Thaller's criticisms and consider those who support the use of relational database systems in historical research Harvey and Press 1996; Champion 1993; Greenstein 1989).

Despite the limitations of desktop databases, it is eminently possible to create a database that cleanly and effectively represents an original historical source. Before a project embarks on actually designing the database itself, it is good practice to consider what the overall relationship between the original paper source and the database is likely to be. As a quick and dirty method for approaching this issue, a number of questions can be asked:

- Does the source have a predominant and consistent structure?
- Are the important items of information relatively well defined, i.e. are they succinct, enclosed elements of information rather than unstructured long textual entries?
- If there are units of measurement (e.g. currency, time/date, dimensions, weight etc.), can they be easily represented for analysis in a database?
- Are there any important non-text, or non-printable characters?
- Is the information itself inconsistent? (Perhaps the most infamous problem is variations in spelling as well as clearly obvious original errors.)

Relational databases are ultimately designed to process structured and consistent data in tabular form. Such software is simply not designed to process large chunks of unstructured text, and in some cases performing transformations or calculations on historical dates or measurements can be overly time consuming. Most modern desktop analysis packages will allow data conversions into additional derived fields without too much pain, and this can be very beneficial to both the initial and potential secondary analysts (Schürer and Oeppen 1990). Creators must make their own judgement on the extent of calculated derived fields.

It should not come as a shock to discover that a significant proportion of historical databases created thus far have been drawn from broadly tabular sources. Poll books, census enumerators' books and reports, registrar general reports, port books and parish registers, are all sources with essentially tabular structures that match with relational databases very well. It is, however, possible to convert other highly structured, but non-tabular, sources into a tabular form whilst retaining the important aspects of the original data. Any project that is serious about creating a digital edition of a source has to make a value judgement about its viability. For a project-focused critique of the relational approach versus other more source-oriented systems see Burt and Beaumont James 1996.

As a broad guide to a source's fitness for tabular database creation, these are some of the qualities in documentary material that may require extra resources or present certain difficulties:

- Unstructured lengthy full-text. (More suitable for 'qualitative' database systems (see Feldman 1995; Kelle 1995; Miles and Huberman 1994), however, some relational systems, such as Filemaker Pro and Oracle, support full-text.)
- Complex or ambiguous units of measurement (e.g. dates rendered in medieval nomenclature can be difficult to use/analyse in standard database packages). Using derived fields is the key here, remembering the possible implications for time.
- Large-scale inconsistencies throughout the source. (Commonly spelling variations, measurement rendering and geographical references.) Section 3.5.2 provides some discussion of these issues.
- Overly complex structures. Ultimately this manifests itself as databases with large numbers of tables and complex (often many-to-many) relationships. Too many tables can make databases daunting and difficult to use.

3.4 SKETCHING THE DATABASE STRUCTURE

Designing and mapping the database structure is one of the most crucial stages of any database creation exercise. This can, and often is, a lengthy process that combines some degree of technical know-how with intellectual decision-making. This section will not go into the specifics of database design – there are many references that project personnel are strongly advised to consult – instead it is intended to provide some broad suggestions for best practice and some advice on the major issues involved.

Perhaps the best starting point for database design, specific to historians, are chapters 1 to 5 in Harvey and Press (1996). Chapter 5 in particular is the best introduction to historical database design published thus far. For more specialist publications on relational databases, database systems and structured query language (SQL), perhaps the most popular is Date (1993) which has gone through a number of editions over the years. In addition, there is an excellent set of web guides about creating and publishing web databases (Scammell 1999).

These rather technical references are useful reading, since any historian who intends to design a database must combine a thorough knowledge of the source material with a fundamental understanding of the potential and limitations of databases and database systems. Database design is ultimately an exercise in methodology.

3.4.1 Sources and tables

For standard relational databases, the design stage concerns translating an historical source, or collection of sources, into an efficient conceptual data model. To simplify the meaning of this process, it could be adequately described as turning sources into tables. It's worth noting that during this process, subjects from one source (e.g. house, person, ship, goods etc.) may form many tables, and it is perfectly possible that subjects across various sources may be collected into single tables. Even if the source material is not *inherently* tabular, a table (or more likely a collection of inter-linked tables) is the format in which the desktop database stores the information. What is under the power of the database designer is not so much the generic structure of the information (which always rests on the premise of rows as records and columns as fields), but rather how the information itself is structured within this matrix strait-jacket. Additionally, whether the source is dismantled into a multitude of related tables and decisions taken about data-types, linking fields and standardisation of values are also primary concerns of the designer.

Unlike some social science datasets, historical tables make sense only when they are precisely defined representations of particular subjects of enquiry, whether taken from single or multiple sources. Databases that contain hundreds of fields in order to fit the data all under one roof are often unwieldy to use and are essentially the product of questionable design. In the same way, databases that contain virtually empty tables are equally as frustrating and inefficient. There is a subtle balance to be achieved between too many or too few tables and too many or too few fields. Database designers have to employ their own sense of what is usable and what is not. Remember that the design of the tables ultimately influences whether the database can be used effectively by both the project itself and further researchers (Harvey and Press 1996, 105–18).

As far as sketching an abstract design is concerned, establishing tables can be done via the 'entity modelling' approach, more formally known as entity relationship modelling (ERM). This is an excellent method for sorting out exactly what sources are going to form what tables, or indeed what parts of the source(s) are going to form tables. This method has the advantage of being a 'top-down' approach and therefore allows the historian to establish an abstract overview of their material and then begin establishing the data entities. Once the entities have been decided upon, the historian can begin a closer examination of these 'meta-tables', which may result in new entities being created and data being restructured in order to create the most efficient and usable database schema. For some examples of this procedure in practice, refer to Acun *et al.* 1994; Harvey and Press 1991; Champion 1993; Poettler 1994 and Scammell 1997.

It is important to keep as detailed a record as possible of the relationship between the database structure and the documentary sources. A comprehensive description of the design model is an essential aid both to the creator(s) and, of course, secondary users. This is an issue of documentation (Chapter 5), but it is important that it is flagged and recognised at an early stage.

3.4.2 Fields and data types

Within database systems tables are made up from fields (sometimes referred to as variables). Highly structured historical documents can also be said to be formed from discrete continuous elements of information – yet reconciling the database field with the element in a source is not necessarily an easy task. This is generally because database systems do have *de facto* limitations on the information that any individual field can hold and these are sometimes not obvious. Historians involved in database creation need to be aware of the potential problems that attempting to squeeze inappropriate data into a field can create. Again, this is as much an issue of common sense as it is of adherence to technical limitations.

Probably the most pressing difficulty with historical sources is that some elements of the data may have rather long textual descriptions or some fields may occasionally have more than a single value associated with them which do not warrant the creation of a separate table. Common examples are multiple occupations, marginal or interpolated notes, and maybe even value changes over time (although this is in a sense a separate issue). Standard database systems do not like these characteristics. Although most database systems will allow textual fields up to a limit of 250 characters, filling up fields in this way is bad practice. Some desktop database packages do allow the incorporation of large textual data into essentially tabular structures, although this is by no means a universal feature. Adding extra fields to compensate for the odd extra value or lengthy textual entry results in an inefficient database. For some examples of real world solutions to these problems, see Schürer and Diederiks (1993). There are some useful strategies for dealing with data that fall outside of standard field specifications, particularly with reference to full-text which can be dealt with using memo fields or even storing the text in separate text files. Using codes and standardisation practices can also overcome some of the limitations imposed by using relational databases (see Section 3.5.2), although potentially they can constitute a significant body of work, the resource implications of which must be considered by any project.

Database fields have another important restriction with regard to data type. Almost all analysis software requires each field in a database to meet a data type specification. Table 1 lists common database data types which may differ slightly from package to package.

Type	Description
Text	Alphanumeric characters, basically anything printable from the keyboard.
Integer	Numbers only (unit separators can often be user defined).
Float	Numbers with decimal points, often referred to as floating point integers.
Memo	Some databases allow full-text memo fields (some cannot be queried however).
BLOB or OLE	Some databases allow using Binary Large Objects for inserting multimedia formats such as images or full documents.
Date	Date format entries. Usually take the form of dd/mm/yyyy. (21/01/1998).
Currency	Essentially as Integer, sometimes with the addition of a currency symbol and decimal places.

Table 1: Common database data types.

The point about data types in relation to historical sources is that they are based on the assumption that the field values will consistently fall within this type. Many database systems will simply fail to work if there is any deviation from this standard. Of course, most source material will not be consistent in this way and database designers must examine their data closely in order to establish where potential pit-falls may occur. By far the most common difficulty occurs with numeric fields. Variables that we may designate as a numeric data type such as 'Age', 'Page Number', 'Population', 'Tonnage', often in real sources contain textual characters. It is usual to find entries such as '5 and a half', '30A', '30569 appx.', or '124tns'. Designers who foresee a need for calculations to be performed on such fields must render them as numeric only.

Good practice with such limitations is to apply consistency that meets with the project objectives and research compass, whilst making documentary notes for future researchers concerning the decisions and judgements made.

3.5 TRANSCRIPTION AND DATA ENTRY

One of the rather irritating aspects of data creation projects is the fact that at some point someone has to 'create' the data. The term 'irritating' is used because the data input stage can be both immensely time consuming and requires attention to detail hitherto unnecessary if the database is to be (largely) error free. The best database design in the world can be utterly destroyed by poor quality data. Although no data collection is perfect, there is a certain quality threshold which, if fallen below, can make a database impossible to use. Most researchers can cope with 'dirty data' but it is up to the creators to minimise the errors. This will make their own research more productive and avoid the need to engage in a massive retrospective correction phase. For a good summary of data entry and validation approaches that supplement this guide, see Harvey and Press 1996, 85–94.

For almost all character-based historical documents (especially hand-written) the only way to transfer information from paper to the computer is through typing. Typing itself can leave an exceptionally large window for human error, and even the most fastidious typists will make mistakes. The transcription process is nothing new to historians, yet it is reasonable to argue that transcribing into a database is a subtly different task which in general requires more accuracy and the use of validation methods. One method for overcoming many of the vexed burdens of historical sources is to apply wide-ranging data standardisation and coding schemes. The application of standards and codes can introduce a high level of accuracy in data, and is more amenable to database system requirements. But such a process also has the potential to be a significant resource consumer which small projects may not be able to accommodate.

3.5.1 Transcription methods

Possibly the best approach to transcription into relational databases is to establish some initial hard rules. In other words, a transcription methodology is constructed in order to tackle some of the ambiguities of historical material and render the database as a consistent and logical whole. The exact nature of the rules and approach will very much depend on the assessment of the original document. There are a number of methods that previous historians using computers have employed, and those creating a resource may want to consider some of these options.

For database creation projects where the intended volume of data is particularly large, transcribing direct from the source into the database can present some difficulties. Also where it is envisaged that some restructuring of the original source will be required and where direct literal transcription is not intended, copying direct from the source document can often be a frustrating experience. One method that may be of particular use is the application of a transcription template. A transcription template is a highly structured form into which the data collector transcribes data from the original source. Templates generally mirror the structure of the end-database and contain easily legible transcriptions that are most useful for cross-referencing and error checking. The large-scale 1881 Census project carried out by the Mormons adopted this method (GSU 1988), other smaller projects have also used transcription templates in order to organise their work (Wakelin and Hussey 1996 and Schürer 1996). The advantages of using a transcription template (for larger projects) could be suggested as follows:

- Allows the data creators to match the template exactly with the database structure.
- Creators can more easily compare the original source with the transcribed copy. Often computer databases can be cumbersome in this respect.
- Allows a 'thinking and decision making' period before the data are entered directly into the computer. Historians can use this time to consider and reflect upon their judgements and can use the template as a filter process.
- When it comes to real data entry, working from a clear template is significantly easier than working from the original.
- Very useful where there are multiple data collectors or where there are two or three levels of transcription checking.

Another method which resource-pressured projects might favour is to use some of the features of the database software itself to assist in data entry and transcription. For example, most database packages will allow the entering of data items to be done via a form interface. A project could develop data entry forms reminiscent of the transcription template described above. Forms should be designed in such a way as to facilitate data entry, allow easy cross-checking, and if there are many tables, allow seamless and intuitive navigation through these.

Quite apart from being easier on the eye than direct data entry into tables, forms can also allow some degree of automated validation. In this way, one can use the restrictiveness of data fields to assist in maintaining accuracy at the data entry stage (Harvey and Press 1996, 130–39). This method can be particularly useful when standardising textual or numerical entries and can be positively invaluable when creating a heavily coded database (see Section 3.5.2). Many popular database systems will allow certain fields only to accept values of a particular data type, data format, or range, sometimes through pull-down menus and look-up tables. For example one could restrict age fields to accept only numeric values, sex fields to accept male, female, or unknown, and date fields to accept only the format dd/mm/yyyy. Also it is possible to apply a more sophisticated level of validation by using look-up tables, hot-key entry and more intelligent input programs. For some instances of such use, see Welling (1993). Although such a method may seem an unnecessary allocation of time and resources, projects should consider very carefully their overall strategy for the data input phase of creation. This is often the forgotten element in resource creation endeavours (probably because of its unglamorous nature). As with most things in database design and creation, effort and thought allocated in the early stages will almost always save time and pay dividends in the long run.

3.5.2 Codes and standardisation

The literature of historians using computers is, unsurprisingly, well represented by publications that tackle the issue of codes and standards. However, what is meant by codes and standards very much depends on the context. For many, what they mean by coding is actually the mark-up coding scheme employed as part of digitising largely textual resources. Also the issue of data standardisation is often referred to as the strategy for data formats in order to facilitate data interchange (see Section 4.3.2). This section, however, will discuss the issue of actually standardising data values and applying coding schemes to data values as a means of overcoming some of the deficiencies of database packages for historical use.

Some historians have always had a rather difficult time dealing with the concept of information standardisation. It is true that to a large extent this has its roots in the belief of the sanctity of the original source and the over-riding necessity never to alter or change it for the purposes of a particular research agenda – essentially the battle between qualitative and quantitative history. This might explain the popularity of the source-oriented methods pioneered by Manfred Thaller and the KLEIO system. The entire raison d'être of such an approach is to keep the source as intact as possible and not hack it to pieces, as is often necessary with standard industry software. For those using standard database applications however, some alteration and editing of the source will almost certainly be necessary in order to prevent the resource being practically unusable. This is an inescapable fact with the vast majority of historical sources (some exceptions being high quality editions or reports).

Standardisation has many benefits if it is carried out with strong principles and sound guidelines. Many historical projects have had to rationalise their data in order to allow record-linkage (Wrigley and Schofield 1973; Bouchard and Pouyez 1980; Davies 1992; Harvey and Press 1996; King 1992), or to map spatial data into GIS software (Silveira et al. 1995, Piotukh 1996 and Southall and Gregory 1998).

No project should feel that this is destroying the provenance of their material; this is a misguided concern, provided that clear and detailed documentation is kept to help alleviate secondary analysts' concerns about methodology and how and why decisions were taken. The nucleus of the problem is that relational database- focused research is best carried out on consistent information. Historical documents are usually rife with inconsistencies and errors and it is natural that in database form these anomalies should be removed. However, the extent of standardisation is an important decision. The rationalisation of obvious spelling variations, date renderings and units of measurement are all justifiable in most cases. When to standardise and when not to is an intellectual decision to be taken either by the single resource creator or by the collective project team (see Wakelin and Hussey 1996, 19). For further references on this issue, including advocacy for post-coding, consult Schürer 1990; Gervers and McCulloch 1990.

Coding data values is probably the ultimate form of data normalisation. It has been common practice in the broader social sciences for many years, and almost all current UK Government surveys are essentially large collections of coded data. In the case of quantitative analysis, coding is often an essential element of data creation. For numerous large-scale historical projects, the use of coded variables has been seen as crucial (Ruggles and Menard 1990). Yet data coding is a resource-intensive process in itself, and projects that deem the application of a coding scheme to be beneficial should be alive to the possible implications. In fact the coding of fields such as occupations is really nothing new and dates back to the later part of the nineteenth century (Booth 1892–1897). Historical computing literature also has a number of articles on this complex problem (Green 1990; Greenstein 1991a; Morris 1990). In a number of projects, coded variables are 'tacked' onto the end of generally textual data tables (Anderson et al. 1979). The advantage of this approach is that it maintains an original textual entry with the cross-reference for analytical purposes of its coded counterpart. Coded data collections are heavily reliant on the quality of accompanying documentation and most particularly on codebooks. Codebooks are essentially guides to the codes which map out the classification scheme used, linking an often numerical code with a textual descriptor. This descriptor is usually either the original entry from the source, or a group classification identifier. Some analysis software (most commonly used statistical packages such as SPSS or Stata) will also allow the designer to define code labels within the application, allowing easy look-up and more meaningful analysis to be performed.

Projects that use codes, particularly those of a highly interpretative nature, are encouraged to document their decisions carefully. In addition to analytical benefits there can also be data entry benefits. The use of abbreviated codes can make the data input stage a faster, more efficient process, especially if an 'intelligent' input form is used. Yet the use of codes can move the database further away from the original source, which has a knock-on effect for the quality level required in documentation. If the project envisages returning to the database after a number of years, or if the data are archived for secondary users, making clear the connections between a heavily normalised data source and the original material it has been extracted from is all the more vital.

Chapter 4 : Further Data and Preservation Issues

4.1 INTRODUCTION

A number of issues have recently begun to make the preservation of digital resources a matter of general concern. This concern has been pushed to the forefront in the light of a number of issues; the most pressing being the realisation that a rapidly digitising world cannot be recorded or preserved using methods which, in some cases, are centuries old and primarily focused on paper archival resources. Those creating new historical digital resources should be aware of the importance of long-term usability and preservation, both for themselves and for potential secondary users.

Data archiving is not particularly new to specialist social scientists. The Data Archive at the University of Essex has been established for over twenty years, with a collection dominated by social science material. Yet for historians the provision of archiving services and facilities is relatively new, beginning formally with the establishment of a history-specific service in 1992. This chapter intends to highlight some broad guidelines to good practice, in order that resource creators may take measures to ensure the long-term usefulness of their data which will ultimately be held by a national data archive. Of necessity, this chapter will take a more technical focus as the key issues involve a relatively detailed discussion of data cleanliness, software problems and data formats. The ability to preserve and share data is at the very centre of the development of a healthy and dynamic computer-using scholarly community. It is the responsibility of data creators to embrace these principles as best that they can.

4.2 DATABASE INTEGRITY AND PRACTICE

Although it is possible to clean and validate a database via data input systems, there is a strong case for retrospective checking so that the database is processed for potential problems, oddities and errors. Errors can slip through even the most stringent of validation procedures. Very often potential problems are not at all obvious. One of the most common difficulties concerns 'special' characters that database systems can often misinterpret as being separate from the data itself. These can create headaches for a project as well as being rather cumbersome for potential secondary analysts. The essential objective is for creators to ensure within resource limits that their data collection is usable and free of extraneous data.

Any correction phase should be relatively short, and this guide will highlight some of the most commonplace problems. Indeed, most difficulties usually arise because of the way in which computers and database systems work rather than any underlying problem with the database itself. Creators should regard this section as a guide to the final stage in checking their data at a micro level in order to prepare these for serious research purposes, or for archiving at a data archive.

4.2.1 Error checking, back-ups and validation

No database is perfectly clean, but some are genuinely cleaner than others. All creation projects should at least factor in some kind of 'post-input' validation scheme. Errors may have slipped through the initial safety net, the project may decide it would be preferable to change the way an aspect of the data is represented, or there may be unforeseen problems which only show themselves after all the hard work of data input has been completed. In some cases errors can seriously affect whether a data collection is usable, but in most instances the errors are generally small and easily fixed.

Databases should be scanned, preferably at regular intervals during the input phase or in a specified time once the input is completed. Any project should make a judgement about the suitability of either approach. This author (ST) has found that interval checking is often the best method simply for the reason that it can draw attention to problems in the embryonic stages, which allow corrective measures to be applied. In one instance, the discovery that the database software had truncated a field from 80 characters to 10 was, thankfully, discovered after the input of only 100 records. The fields had to be re-entered but the cost was minimal because of the policy of regular data checks. Software can sometimes be unpredictable and data can be lost or corrupted for a host of unknown reasons.

Because of the somewhat unstable nature of both software and hardware systems, all validation procedures should be accompanied by a comprehensive and sensible back-up procedure (Harvey and Press 1996, 37). There have in the past, and will probably continue to be, horror stories of projects losing either all or large chunks of their data which could not be replaced because no back-up methodology was employed. Some key principles to remember:

- Back-up your database regularly.
- If possible, back it up in both the format of the used software and in a neutral format such as ASCII.
- Back-up data to a medium that is entirely isolated from the principal hardware currently being used. If it is possible to back-up data to floppy disk, CD-ROM, magnetic tape or a networked device, then do.
- It may seem excessive, but it is wise to back-up the back-ups. Check that the copies are actually usable and avoid continuous over-writing of old back-ups with new ones in case the new files are corrupted.

Network crashes, software bugs, or virus infections can all destroy what is ultimately a volatile resource. Needless to say, it is in the interests of the project and the wider research community that digital resources are protected from such disasters.

Validation should be a systematic process. It is fairly simple, if tedious, to apply some checks to databases using database query functions (either SQL or forms-based queries) (Morrison 1989). Databases can be examined for errors table by table if necessary but not all fields may be appropriate for checking. As a general processing rule, fields for which we expect certain limited value ranges to occur are the most important. These are the ones where anomalies are easy to identify and subsequently correct. Also, data collections that contain coded variables are simple to check (if the input stage is not foolproof). One possible method for relational systems is to construct a query that uses a GROUP and COUNT function (see Harvey and Press 1996, 159). This would assemble a list of the values of a particular field and count the occurrences of each one. Much the same as a frequency count, this would allow for the identification of outliers or erroneous entries. Of course, this will not indicate if a value within the particular range has been typed in error. If the project is keen to iron out all possible mistakes, then some cross-corroboration with the original source will be required.

4.2.2 Common problems

Some problems of data integrity can be tough to spot. It is also important to warn that some characters and combinations of characters can result in database systems not exporting or importing data correctly. It is unfortunate, but hardly surprising, that these special characters often occur in historical sources. In addition, computers also use a number of characters such as spaces, tabs or end-of-lines that are not always immediately visible. When preparing data for deposit with a data archive, creators are advised to ensure that their data will not present difficulties in importing or exporting from one software system to another (see Section 4.3.2 for a more detailed discussion).

Table 2 describes the main special characters over which database creators are advised to take care. Many of the potential pit-falls can be avoided if it is recognised where and when special characters are used. In particular, special characters can become a problem when data is exported to an ASCII data format. ASCII data formats are important for preservation purposes, but database systems can assign special, and originally unintended meanings to special characters when importing data from ASCII files. A very common problem is extraneous space characters that may occur at the beginning or end of a field entry or may have been double typed (i.e. two consecutive spaces). These should be cleaned up as they can present problems when querying data. For example an entry in an occupation field such as ' Farmer' (with a leading space) will

Character	Problem
Quote marks (" or ')	Many popular database systems use quote marks as a means of establishing a text type field. If there are quote marks in the source that should be retained then beware.
Commas (,)	Used to separate field entries in comma separated ASCII format.
Tabs	Used to separate field entries in tab delimited ASCII format.
Newlines	Generally should never be used within a relational database field entry. Most database systems see newlines as the beginning of a new record.
Spaces	Some (few) database systems use spaces to delimit field entries. The major problem with spaces is when they occur at the beginning or end of textual fields in error. Database string matching queries will pick these up and may present unexpected/incomplete results.
Extended ASCII and foreign characters	Although ASCII now supports characters in a variety of other languages, it is not certain whether all database systems support this. Caution is to be taken with extended ASCII and systems should preferably be thoroughly tested.

Table 2: Common problem characters.

not be picked up by a query asking for matches of 'Farmer' (no leading space). The origin of such problems is that databases, unless told otherwise, match the input query strings *exactly* with values in the database itself. Therefore, if by accident tabs or spaces have been entered into a field, the database query will not pick these entries up unless it is specifically instructed to ignore such anomalies. One of the best workarounds is to use wildcard values or 'approximate' matching such as the 'LIKE' function in SQL.

Another issue pertinent to historical databases is the use of null (blank) entries and the method by which the database creator has indicated a transcription difficulty. The key here is to establish firm rules as part of the overall transcription process (Section 3.3.1). Despite what one might naturally assume, database systems are quite happy dealing with blank entries. Indeed, most good systems (especially those based on SQL) recognise a blank field easily. There are, however, a number of examples of historical databases where, instead of using a null entry, the designer has opted to identify blank fields with the use of a special character or string. Common usage includes "-", "—", or "blank" (GSU and FFHS 1997). This approach does unfortunately have the propensity to create more difficulties than it solves, particularly if there is a general lack of consistency. As a generic guideline, creators are encouraged to leave null entries as null (i.e. empty) rather than using any particular character or string to represent this.

A different, and more complex, issue is the problem of uncertain transcription. Historians using computers are well aware of this dilemma and a number of approaches have been adopted in order to address this aspect of databases (GSU and FFHS 1997). In much the same way as dealing with nulls, creators are strongly advised to establish a framework and methodology for tackling partial or uncertain transcription during the database *design* stage. The rules have to be in place before transcription begins (with all transcribers aware of these rules) in order that consistency is maintained. Moreover, consistency is vital for immediate analysts of the data source and future scholars.

Two common approaches to this issue are to use some sort of confidence weighting indicator, or a tag that identifies when a data value has been transcribed with some uncertainty. The first approach attaches a statistical measure of confidence to a particular entry where there has been some difficulty in transcription. An example might be to use a weight from 0 (no confidence) to 1 (full confidence) as documented by Thaller (1993). In relational database systems this may not be a particularly elegant solution, as it may involve adding mostly redundant fields to a table. The design of a 'transcription look-up table' (a separate table linked by a unique identifier with fields indicating the field name and weighting factor) might be a workable approach. Certainly the use of tags can be a rather inelegant workaround. Databases that use character-based tags to indicate transcription anomalies tend not to work particularly well. The use of question marks or brackets to draw attention to problematic entries can be confusing, especially in cases where the source itself includes question marks and brackets. If a database is to include a relatively detailed set of indicators of transcription confidence then this should be thought over carefully and should be implemented consistently.

4.3 SOFTWARE, FORMATS AND PRESERVATION STANDARDS

All data creation projects will rely on some sort of software application, whether a simple text editor or full-scale relational database management system. The software used has significant implications for phases of the project from data entry to analysis, and may also affect issues of data formats and therefore preservation standards. Sensible decisions about software and data formats will have beneficial effects not only for the project itself but also for the capacity for future reuse of the resource.

This section will provide some broad guidelines for software selection, use of data formats, and preservation criteria. Many of the suggestions are common sense, although decisions concerning the applicability of particular data formats and methods ensuring that a resource is 'preservation friendly' are largely technical issues. It is important to reiterate that a project that has considered these challenges early on will almost certainly be in an excellent position to meet adequate standards. The pressures placed on research and the frequently expedient nature of resource creation mean that the issue of data preservation is often ignored. Preservation is, however, one of the most important aspects of any resource creation project and deserves considerable attention (Anderson 1992; Higgs 1992).

4.3.1 Software selection

The choice of inappropriate software can severly hamper any type of project. Software selection is usually limited by the choices available within a particular institution, as projects are very rarely funded for overheads such as major software purchases. At the time of writing there are many database systems on the market although the dominance of the Microsoft standard is clear and unequivocal. Despite this *de facto* standard, there are many database applications installed on university systems or researcher's workstations that appear 'fit for purpose'. This section provides some introductory guidelines about the desired elements of database software that are conducive to the successful completion of project objectives.

A primary consideration is the data capacity of any particular system. A project that envisages the creation of a database of upwards of 100,000 records should research the data-handling capacity of its intended software. Even if the hardware platform has adequate resources, some software products place a limit on the number of records in each table. In general, it is spreadsheet software and not database software that usually imposes record limits (Microsoft Excel, for example, imposes a record limit). However, some database systems, particularly PC-based ones, do struggle to cope with large and complex databases even if no record limit is forced. This is due to the resource-intensive nature of desktop operating systems such as Windows95, Windows98 and MacOS. Larger scale projects are strongly advised to use a UNIX platform or the Windows NT operating system. Table 3

Small- to Medium-Scale Projects Windows 95/98	Larger Scale Projects UNIX variants and Windows NT
Paradox	ORACLE
FoxPro	INGRES
Access	SQL Server
Dbase	SAS
File Maker Pro	

Table 3: Operating systems and database software.

gives a rudimentary summary of the most popular database applications with their associated operating systems. For examples of smaller scale projects using Dbase, consult Champion (1993) and Hatton *et al.* (1997). The general rule is that if a project estimates that there may be significant resource implications with their database, then using a UNIX-based software system is a safer option. Naturally, migrating platforms halfway through a project is to be avoided, yet employing some of the guidelines highlighted in this chapter should make such migration possible.

As well as handling the data, the software must provide the tools that are crucial for the creation and management of the digital resource. These tools can be classified as follows: Database Design, Data Entry, Validation and Data Query. Database software in general supports these elements, it is simply a question of *how* each particular package approaches individual functions. The most obvious differences in implementations are between SQL-based database systems, non-SQL-based systems, and those (SQL or otherwise) with graphical user interfaces. As a rule, SQL-based systems (particularly of the UNIX variety) tend to be targeted more at large-scale corporate databases and are, as a result, generally more flexible and powerful, with the emphasis on the management system. They are also designed as 'mission critical' applications with associated improvements in robustness. Recent versions of Microsoft Access and SQL Server combine SQL with the functionality of a Windows-based user interface. For those who envisage networking capabilities, systems with ODBC compliance are very useful – particularly for remote access to a central data store. As a broad guideline it is suggested that projects opt for a database system that supports SQL functions and conventions. For an excellent brief article in using SQL in an historical context see Burnard (1989), also Harvey and Press (1994).

The database software application should support all the types of data that the project intends to digitise and provide a comprehensive array of export formats. For projects that plan to use full text entries, and incorporate them into the database as a whole, only systems that support either full text processing or memo fields are appropriate. In some cases, historians may perceive the need to use more specialised software applications in addition to the core database system. This might ultimately involve migrating the data (or subsets of the data) into other applications, such as statistical software or Geographical Information System (GIS) databases. It therefore pays well for the project to investigate in some detail the supported export formats of their database in combination with the import formats of the proposed second application. If such data transference is likely to be common, then the purchase of a special data migration tool such as StatTransfer or DBMSCopy might be profitable. Even with today's sophisticated software, one particular database's export formats may not match the secondary software's import formats. This is quite apart from the fact that a number of problems and anomalies can occur while transferring data from one format to the other. The bottom line is: if in doubt, test, and double test, before the project begins in earnest.

4.3.2 The importance of data formats

Very often data formats are the forgotten aspect of database creation projects. Generally little thought goes into data formats beyond that which is relevant to the core database software application. However, data interchange is an important consideration and this depends almost exclusively on the data format in which the data are available. Try importing an SPSS portable file or SAS transport file into either Access or Excel and the point becomes clear. In much the same way, the ASCII data from programs such as KLEIO or Idealist are not necessarily suitable for any other application.

Suitable data formats are primarily important for data interchange and data preservation. Specialist interchange programs such as StanFEP (Thaller 1988a) have been developed in the past, although the use of such systems (despite their sound theory) has not been popularly adopted. Creators should consider these issues in relation to their own databases, both as a precursor for future preservation and also as a means to maintain some degree of flexibility with their data source. The key is maintaining a 'neutral' format of the database. A neutral format is one that maintains level of independence between data and software allowing digital resources to be preserved even after the original software has become obsolete. Indeed it is because of a lack of thought about independence between data and associated software that so many scholarly digital resources are now being lost.

It is possible to distinguish between two broad classes of data. One is ASCII data, the other is binary data. The importance of this distinction for database creators is that ASCII data are generally easier to share between applications than binary data. This is because ASCII is about the only *de facto* non-proprietary data standard currently adopted in computing. Almost all software packages will accept ASCII data in one form or the other, whereas the ability to import a particular binary software-specific format varies from application to application. Data creators are encouraged to learn about how ASCII works and to use it as a supported data format for their databases. The import and export of ASCII-based data files is supported by nearly all database systems.

Unfortunately there are subtle differences between DOS-based ASCII and UNIX-based ASCII which present further complications. The characters themselves are drawn from the same ASCII table, but the end-of-line character (i.e. the value representing a carriage return) has been implemented differently in each system. Creators should be aware that migration of ASCII data from a UNIX platform to a DOS/Windows platform (and vice-versa) must employ the use of a conversion program in order to convert the end of line characters. Ultimately, any transfers of this type must be tested to ensure that they have been successful. For a summary of this problem and further data format issues see Wright 1997.

Resource creators must think carefully about which formats their database can support. For tabular databases the data structure is at least non-problematic. The challenge is whether a complex database system can be rendered into an essentially ASCII form with no loss of intrinsic information. This may have implications for documentation, as guides to reconstructing the database are often necessary. In addition, any special software-specific programs would have to be abandoned and it is therefore important that such programs are not crucial to the usability of the data. Historians should consider the extent to which their data source is completely independent from any particular piece of software.

4.3.3 Preservation standards

The cliometric historian Emmanuel Le Roy Ladurie commented in 1979 that 'Tomorrow's historian will have to be able to programme [sic] a computer in order to survive' (Evans 1997, 19). One could add to this statement that 'computer-based historical research can only flourish if the resources survive'. Preservation has hitherto been the forgotten element of digital resource creation projects – large or small. This section will introduce some important guidelines to best practice for preservation.

Firstly, it would be wrong to see preservation practices as simply a nod to secondary analysts. The creators also have much to gain from the application of good practices. Consider the analogy of producing a paper scholarly volume, all copies of which are primed to self-destruct within two years. Gone, therefore, are the possibilities of returning to the resource for future reference, incorporating the data in new research, or revising findings and updating information as new research progresses. Much of the power and value of digital data resources comes from the ease with which they can be reused in these ways. Material that has been created without any concessions to preservation standards could, however, face being consigned to the digital waste bin within a relatively short period of time. This is as much a concern for the creators of the database as it is for anyone else.

As suggested in Section 4.3.2, ASCII is really the only *de facto* cross-platform data standard available at the present time. This rather sad fact is indicative of the short-term focus present throughout the computer industry. Data standards other than ASCII represent the current position of a particular software application in the overall market place, or at least the general popularity of a software application among data users. These formats are usually binary in nature and although some of them have been established over ten years or more, there are no guarantees that such resources could be preserved for an unspecified time-span. From a preservation perspective, the problem with a binary format is that it runs the risk of becoming unreadable owing to unforeseen circumstances. It is a reality of life in the computer industry that software companies come and go, software formats become updated (sometimes with no backwards compatibility), applications change their supported formats (how many applications supported HTML in the mid 1990s?), and once fashionable solutions to a data problem can be replaced with an improved method leaving supporters of the old solution high and dry.

The HDS has considerable expertise in dealing with formats for historical material. Table 4 indicates the formats that the HDS recognises as being suitable for deposit. The suggested binary formats simply represent current standards today, although they are *not* standards in the strictest sense. All of these applications have gone through a number of versions over recent years. The HDS as a general rule favours the latest versions of the software at any given moment in time. The rationale is that such software-specific formats can easily be migrated to

ASCII	Binary Software Specific
Comma separated variables	Access
Tab delimited variables	Dbase (not strictly binary)
Fixed width	Paradox
SQL definitions and set-ups	FoxPro
Other delimited variables	Excel
	Lotus 1–2–3
	Quattro Pro

Table 4: Supported database formats for deposit with the HDS.

a neutral ASCII format for preservation purposes. Most of the above software formats are generally interchangeable, especially in relation to Microsoft products. In most cases the HDS will maintain both a binary and ASCII form of the database if the initial deposit has been non-ASCII. Resource creators should avoid at all costs the use of very specific software features. These usually include special programs using a proprietary language, macros, menu systems, or other software-specific features that strongly influence the use of the database and cannot be replicated.

Historians should ensure that their databases meet what are essentially *de facto* data-sharing standards. The best way to achieve this objective is via the use of ASCII data copies, specifically aimed towards a preservation-ready duplicate. Almost all popular desktop database systems will export as ASCII, and SQL-based systems can export tables according to a user-defined specification. Whilst creators may feel uneasy deconstructing their databases in this way, it is really of no consequence as long as the database can be successfully reconstructed. The responsibility for establishing materials that are re-usable lies with the creator. A data archive can only work with what is deposited. Ultimately the role of a data archive is to ensure the long-term usefulness of a resource by the implementation of a preservation strategy which takes account of changing technical regimes and environments. At the outset, however, it is the resource creator who determines the likely life span of the material.

Chapter 5 : Documenting a Data Creation Project

5.1 WHY IS GOOD DOCUMENTATION IMPORTANT?

The maintenance of comprehensive documentation detailing the data creation process and the steps taken involves a significant but profitable investment of time and resources. It is more effective if documentation is generated during, rather than after, a data creation project. Such an approach will result in a better-quality data collection, as well as better-quality documentation, because the maintenance of proper documentation demands consistency and attention to detail. The process of documenting a data creation project can also have the benefit of helping to refine research questions and it can be a vital aid to communication in larger projects.

Good documentation is crucial to a data collection's long-term vitality; without it, the resource will not be suitable for future use and its provenance will be lost. Proper documentation contributes substantially to a data collection's scholarly value. The elements essential to good documentation are described in Section 5.2. At a minimum, documentation should provide information about a data collection's contents, provenance and structure, and the terms and conditions that apply to its use. It needs to be sufficiently detailed to allow the data creator to use the resource in the future, when the data creation process has started to fade from memory. It also needs to be comprehensive enough to enable others to explore the resource fully, and detailed enough to allow someone who has not been involved in the data creation process to understand the data collection and the process by which it was created.

5.2 GUIDELINES FOR DOCUMENTING A DATA CREATION PROJECT

5.2.1 Contents

A description of the contents of the data collection should be provided in sufficient detail to allow any potential user to assess whether it is suitable for their needs. This factual description should include, where applicable:

- Title, which describes the contents and gives an indication of the temporal and geographic coverage.
- Main types of information it contains.
- Strengths and weaknesses.
- Time period(s) covered, including details of any data which only partially cover the time period.

- Periodicity of the data collection (e.g. monthly, annual, decennial).
- Name(s) of the country, region, county, town or village covered. If the names or the administrative units were different during the time period covered by the data collection, document those names or administrative units and their present-day equivalents.
- Types of spatial units that can be used to analyse the data collection.
- Language(s) used.

5.2.2 Provenance

The provenance of a data collection needs to be documented in detail. This information should include how, why, when and by whom the data collection was created and used.

Who created the data collection and why?
A data collection's intellectual context should be documented thoroughly enough to enable someone who has not been involved in the project to understand the intellectual framework in which it was created. This information should include:

- Other title(s) and reference number(s) that have been used to identify the data collection during the data creation process.
- Name(s), affiliation(s) and role(s) of all the individual(s) or organisation(s) who have been involved in the data creation process.
- Names of any organisation(s) or individual(s) that funded the creation of the data collection, with grant numbers and titles where appropriate.
- Description and history of the research project (or other process) which gave rise to the data collection, including the main aims, objectives and topics of research.
- Description and history of how the data collection has been used.
- Bibliographic references for any publications based upon or about the data collection.
- Bibliographic references to any related data collections.

How was the data collection created?
The way in which a data collection was created should be described in sufficient detail to allow any potential user to understand the steps that were taken. This information should include:

- How and why the methods used and the structure and format of the data collection were chosen.
- Hardware and software used to create the data collection, and whether it has at any point been converted to new systems or formats.
- Dates relating to the creation of the data collection, including any dates when it was significantly amended.

Which sources were used to create the data collection?
Detailed information about the source(s) used to create the data collection should be provided so that any user can trace the data collection back to its original source(s) and understand the relationship between the data collection and the source(s). This information should include:

- List of sources, including archival or bibliographic references.
- Purpose, scope, content, provenance, administration and history of the source(s), including

any unusual or inconsistent features such as the destruction or separation of parts of the source.
- Bibliographic references to works that describe the source(s).
- Details of how the source(s) have been converted to digital form, including: completeness of transcription, sampling and selection methods, standardisation procedures, and the use of mark-up, classification and coding schemes.
- Details of the relationship between the data collection and the source(s) including a photocopy or image of each source, with an example showing how it is represented in the data collection.

5.2.3 Structure

It is essential that the structure, form and organisation of a data collection be described fully. This information should include:

- List of files and tables with information about their contents, number of records and fields, and the way in which they relate both to each other and to the source.
- List of field names used in each file with information about the characteristics of each field, including name, contents, field length, data type and any codes used, and information about the way in which the fields relate to each other and to the source, including details of derived variables.
- Format of the data collection, including the delimiters used in delimited ASCII files.

5.2.4 Terms and conditions

It is important that all the terms and conditions that apply to the use of a data collection are fully documented. In particular, copyright and other intellectual property rights must be clearly established, and the name(s) of the copyright holder(s) both for the data collection and for the original source material must be specified. If the collection was created during your work as an employee, the copyright holder will normally be your employer under your contract of employment. In particular, give full details if copyright is held jointly, if there are multiple copyrights, or if the collection is covered by Crown copyright. For further information about copyright see AHDS and TASI (1999).

Chapter 6 : Archiving and Preserving Data

6.1 WHAT IS THE HISTORY DATA SERVICE?

A major theme of this guide is the importance of creating digital resources that are suitable for archiving and re-use. The History Data Service (HDS) collects high-quality digital resources – transcribed, scanned or compiled from historical source documents – which are of long-term interest to the historical community. The collection covers a wide range of historical topics, and brings together over 450 separate collections of data, including databases, spreadsheets, textbases, texts and scanned images. Data collections are accessioned for all periods, from ancient history through to 1945, and although the primary focus is on the UK, cross-national data collections are regularly accessioned. Data are accepted in a variety of formats, including delimited ASCII, ASCII texts in particular SGML marked-up texts, databases, spreadsheets and images, and on a variety of media including CD-ROMs, disks and cartridge tapes, as well as via FTP. The HDS *Collections Development Policy* contains further information about the scope and the nature of the collection, and Section 6.3 contains further information about preferred and acceptable data formats.

The HDS preserves digital resources produced by individuals, projects and organisations, mainly within the higher education sector. It is supported in this effort by the Arts and Humanities Research Board, Humanities Research Board of the British Academy, the Economic and Social Research Council, the Leverhulme Trust and the Wellcome Trust's History of Medicine Programme. All of these funding bodies either require or recommend that their grantholders offer for deposit with the HDS any historical digital data that they may produce. Where significant bodies of historical data are managed by other agencies, such as other data centres and data archives, the HDS negotiates data exchange and/or access agreements in preference to direct acquisition.

Data are deposited with the HDS with a non-exclusive licence for use in research and teaching. This means that intellectual property rights and copyright are retained by the copyright holder(s) and that the depositor grants the HDS the necessary permissions to preserve and disseminate the data for research and teaching.

6.2 WHAT ARE THE BENEFITS OF DEPOSITING DATA WITH THE HDS?

6.2.1 Ensuring preservation

The time and resources invested in the creation of digital resources can easily be placed in jeopardy because hardware and software become obsolete, and magnetic media degrade. Long-term preservation is essential if this investment is to be safeguarded. Data collections deposited with the HDS are preserved and migrated through changing technologies to ensure that they will be accessible in the future.

6.2.2 Providing access

Many historical digital resources have significant and long-term value to the research and teaching community, and the time and resources invested in their creation can only be fully realised if they are systematically collected, preserved and disseminated. The HDS makes deposited data collections available for future re-use, distributing them to the research and teaching community in a range of formats and on a variety of media. Data collections deposited with the HDS are professionally catalogued, and information about them and any associated publications is made accessible through online catalogues.

6.2.3 Professional recognition

By collecting, evaluating, cataloguing and publicising data collections, the HDS helps to provide tangible evidence of the scholarly effort involved in data creation. Data collections deposited with the HDS are widely publicised, for example through workshops and online catalogues, and individual depositors gain professional recognition when their data collections are re-used in research and teaching and cited in subsequent publications.

6.3 STEP-BY-STEP GUIDE TO DEPOSITING DATA WITH THE HDS

1. *Contact the HDS to check that your data is suitable for deposit and to obtain the necessary forms.*
2. *Produce copies of all the data files in a neutral machine-independent format, preferably either as software-independent files with data definition files (e.g. tab delimited or comma separated ASCII files) or as export files (e.g. SPSS export files).*

    Data files can be accepted in a variety of formats as long as they are machine-independent and fully described in the *Data and Documentation Transfer Form*. Software-independent files with data definition files or export files are preferable; however, software-dependent files can be accepted if full details of the software are supplied in the *Data and Documentation Transfer Form* (please contact the HDS in advance to check whether the software in question is supported). Preferred and acceptable data formats are listed in Table 5. If you are uncertain about which format is most appropriate for the deposit of your data, please do not hesitate to contact the HDS. Data can be sent to the HDS via FTP, floppy disk, dat tape, exabyte tape, 6150 'QIC' tape, CD-ROM, or, by arrangement, via other media.
3. *Produce copies of all the documentation, preferably as Word files. However, WordPerfect, SGML marked up text and ASCII files are also acceptable. If computer-readable files are not available, then please provide clean paper copies suitable for photocopying.*

    The documentation that accompanies a data collection deposited with the HDS should meet the standards set out in Section 5.2. It should be comprehensive enough to allow

Type of Data	Preferred Formats	Acceptable Formats
Databases	Delimited ASCII (tab delimited variables, comma separated variables (CSV), or other delimited variables), Fixed width ASCII	SQL definitions and set-ups, Access, Dbase, FoxPro, Paradox
Images	TIF, PNG, SPIFF	GIF, BMP
Spreadsheets	Delimited ASCII (tab delimited variables, comma separated variables (CSV), or other delimited variables), Fixed width ASCII	Excel, Lotus 1–2–3, Quattro Pro
Statistical Packages	Delimited ASCII (tab delimited variables, comma separated variables (CSV), or other delimited variables) with SPSS set-up file or SIR schema, Fixed width ASCII with SPSS set-up file or SIR schema	SPSS portable, SIR export, STATA export, SAS transport (with separate ASCII file listing variable value labels)
Texts	ASCII, SGML	RTF, HTML, Word, WordPerfect, PDF

Table 5: Preferred and acceptable data formats

someone who has not been involved in the data creation process to understand the data and the process by which they were created. In exceptional cases, data collections which are not accompanied by comprehensive documentation may be considered for deposit after negotiation and agreement.

4. *Complete a Data and Documentation Transfer Form*
    The *Data and Documentation Transfer Form* is used to obtain all the essential information about the physical transfer of your data and documentation to the HDS. If you have any difficulty completing it, please do not hesitate to contact the HDS.

5. *Complete a Catalogue Form*
    The information that you provide on the *Catalogue Form* will be used to produce a full catalogue record for online catalogues. Please take care when completing this form, because online catalogues are the principal mechanism through which users will discover information about your data collection, and it is you who are best placed to ensure that this information is accurate. We will be happy to update the catalogue record for you if, for example, additions need to be made to the list of associated publications. If you have any difficulty completing this form, please do not hesitate to contact the HDS.

6. *Complete and sign a Licence Form*
    Data are deposited with the HDS with a non-exclusive licence use in research and teaching. This means that intellectual property rights and copyright are retained by the copyright holder(s) and that the depositor grants the HDS the necessary permissions to preserve and disseminate the data for use in research and teaching. You can only deposit data and grant these permissions if you are the copyright holder or are authorised to do so by the copyright holder(s). Copyright and other intellectual property rights must be clearly

established before a data collection is deposited. The HDS can offer advice and guidance about clearing intellectual property rights and copyright.

7.   *Complete a Checklist Form*
     The *Checklist Form* provides a means for you quickly to check that you are supplying everything that the HDS needs to accession your data collection. The HDS will return your transfer medium to you if you request this on the *Checklist Form*.

8.   *Send the data, documentation and forms to the History Data Service, Data Archive, University of Essex, Colchester, CO4 3SQ, preferably by registered post, or contact the HDS to arrange an FTP transfer.*

6.4 FURTHER INFORMATION

Staff at the HDS will be happy to answer any queries you may have about creating, documenting and depositing data and can provide you with information about HDS training courses. If your interest is in arts, humanities or social science data, rather than historical data *per se*, please contact either the appropriate Arts and Humanities Data Service Service Provider or the Data Archive. If you are in doubt regarding the appropriate AHDS service provider, please contact the AHDS Executive in the first instance. For contact details please see the inside cover.

Chapter 7 : Glossary and Bibliography

7.1 GLOSSARY

Access	A widely used relational database system part of the Microsoft Office suite.
AHDS	Arts and Humanities Data Service.
ASCII	American Standard Code for Information Interchange. An international standard allowing computers to exchange and display character-based data. Most relational database systems can import and export ASCII data in a number of delimited ASCII data formats.
Binary	Data that do not adhere to a character coding scheme such as ASCII or EBCDIC. Binary format data can only be read with specific software packages usually on specific computer platforms.
BMP	BitMaP. A widely used graphic image format common in Windows applications.
Case	See record. Terminology usually associated with statistical analysis.
CCTA	Central Computer and Telecommunications Agency http://www.ccta.gov.uk/cctahome.htm
CEBs	Census Enumerators Books
Codes	A popular method of associating textual values with numeric codes. Most important for classifying complex data in order to facilitate meaningful analysis. The most common coding framework in historical data (and contemporary data) applies to the classification and categorisation of occupations.
Comma Separated ASCII	Also known as CSV or Comma Separated Values. An ASCII data format where each field in a record is separated by a comma character.
Critical Path	The longest 'distance' or time to complete a project. If any activity on the critical path takes longer than planned, the end date of the project slips accordingly.
Data Format	Refers to the way in which the contents of a data file are organised. Many data formats are specific to one software application. Comma separated and tab delimited ASCII are common formats which can be read by many analysis packages and into standard text editors. Most desktop database systems are able to read data from a number of formats.
Data Model	The theoretical model by which data are structured. Common data models include relational, network, hierarchical and object-oriented. Data

	modelling is a methodology for structuring data for use in a database system. See also ERM and RDA.
Data Type	A database system term that is used to define the characteristic of a particular field. The system will then expect all values in this field to conform to given rules on this type, i.e. numeric types cannot contain word characters.
Database	A generic term commonly used to describe a structured collection of data. Databases can take many forms including unstructured full text, images, maps, statistics or a mixture of data sources. For this guide, the term database refers to essentially tabular data containing text and numbers.
Database System	The software application that the user employs to define, create, manage and analyse a database. This guide is concerned with relational database systems primarily, although these are by no means the only type of database system software available.
Dbase	A widely used relational database system.
Delimited ASCII	An ASCII data format where each field in a record is separated by a specified character e.g. comma or tab.
Deliverable	An item which the project has to create as part of the requirements. It may be part of the final outcome or an intermediate element on which one or more subsequent deliverables are dependent. According to the type of project, another name for a deliverable is 'product'.
ERM	Entity Relationship Modelling. A methodology for designing a database. Used to specify what entities are of interest and in what ways these entities are linked. A finalised entity will form a table in the database itself and its attributes will form fields.
Excel	A widely used spreadsheet package part of the Microsoft Office suite.
Export	A facility provided by most database systems to convert or export data into a different data format.
Field	A precise element of information within a table taking the form of a column. Sometimes referred to as a variable in statistical analysis.
Fixed Width ASCII	An ASCII data format where each field in a record begins at a set column position and has a set width.
Flat-File	Describes data that are structured (modelled) into one single table.
Form	A common on-screen interface to databases allowing users to enter data, maintain data and query data within the database system. Often used to avoid complex SQL commands and to automate some database processes.
FoxPro	A widely used relational database system.
FTP	File Transfer Protocol
GIF	Graphics Interchange Format. A widely used graphic image format owned by CompuServe.
GIS	Geographical Information System. A database system that links digital maps with attribute data, usually tabular in structure. Provides powerful and complex tools to visualise and analyse data in a spatial context.

HDS	History Data Service
HTML	HyperText Markup Language. A widely used document format. HTML uses tags as part of a general framework for describing a document structure primarily for the World Wide Web.
Import	A facility provided by most database systems to convert or import data into the database system's standard data format.
Lotus 1–2–3	A widely used spreadsheet package part of the Lotus SmartSuite.
Media	The storage medium used to hold data. Common examples include CD-ROM, DAT, DVD-ROM, Floppy disk Hard disk and Magnetic Tape.
Model-Oriented	A methodology used by historians in order to fit their sources into a structured data model, usually resulting in some loss or restructuring of information. Commonly associated with the application of the relational data model.
Null	A term used mainly within database systems, SQL and programming languages, to indicate that a field has no value. This is subtly, but importantly different, from assigning a value which means 'blank', 'empty' or 'no data'.
Paradox	A widely used relational database system.
PDF	Portable Document Format. A widely used document format promoted by Adobe.
Platform	A term that defines both the operating system of the computer and its hardware base, usually referring to the central processing unit. For example, the most common computing platform today is Windows/Intel Pentium.
PNG	Portable Network Graphics. Pronounced 'ping'. A relatively new graphic image format.
PRINCE	PRojects IN Controlled Environments; a method which supports some selected aspects of project management.
Quattro Pro	A widely used spreadsheet package.
RDA	Relational Data Analysis. A methodology for designing a database from the bottom-up. Used to isolate each discrete item of information which are then normalised and restructured to form entities. Designed to remove data duplication and data redundancy.
RDBMS	Relational Database Management System. See database system.
Record	A complete item of information within a table taking the form of a row. Contains one or more descriptive fields and is usually a list of subjects, e.g. people, places, goods, items, etc.
Record-Linkage	Refers to the computer-based procedure of linking records from (often) different sources. The most common example is nominal record-linkage which is a methodology for linking people across time from different sources, based on their names and other attributes. Popular with prosopographers.
Relational	Describes a particular type of data model which structures data into individual tables, each made up of fields which are linked together (related) through a system of key fields.

Risk	The chance of exposure to the adverse consequences of future events.
RTF	Rich Text Format. A widely used document format.
SAS	A widely used statistical package.
SAS Transport	Export format for SAS.
SGML	Standard Generalised Mark-up Language. A widely used document format. SGML uses tags as part of a general framework for describing a document structure.
SIR	A widely used statistical package.
SIR Export	Export format for SIR.
SIR Schema	A series of SIR commands which define a database's structure.
Slack	In relation to project activities, slack or slack time means that there is more time available to complete an activity than needed. Activities with slack are not on the critical path.
Source-Oriented	A methodology used by historians to create databases that are able to represent every single aspect of the original source material without loss. Often associated with the concept of the critical edition advocated by Manfred Thaller. The database system KLEIO is commonly understood to be source-oriented.
SPIFF	Still Picture Interchange File Format. A relatively new graphic image format.
SPSS	A widely used statistical package.
SPSS Portable	Export format for SPSS which is the best way to transfer SPSS data files from one type of machine to another. Variable names, variable labels, value labels, formats, and missing-value specifications are saved along with the data.
SPPS Set-up	A series of SPSS commands which define a database's structure.
SQL	Structured Query Language. A computer language developed for use with relational database systems. Has an extensive set of commands that allow the user to define, manage and analyse/query the database. Most desktop applications now include an SQL component.
SQL Definitions and Set-ups	A series of SQL commands which define a database's structure.
Stage	A division of a project for management purposes. According to PRINCE, a 'Project Board' approves the project to proceed one stage at a time.
Stata	A widely used statistical package.
Stata Export	Export format for Stata.
Tab Delimited ASCII	An ASCII data format where each field in a record is separated (delimited) by a tab character.
Table	A complete table of information within a database.
TIF	Tagged Interchange File Format. TIF (PC) or TIFF (Macintosh). A widely used graphic image format.
Variable	See field.
Word	A widely used word-processing package part of the Microsoft Office suite.
WordPerfect	A widely used word-processing package.

7.2 BIBLIOGRAPHY

Acun, R., Anane, R. and Laflin, S., 1994. Database design for Ottoman tax registers. In: H.J. Marker and K. Pagh (eds.) *Yesterday. Proceedings from the 6th international conference Association of History and Computing Odense 1991.* Odense: Odense University Press, 109–23.

AHDS and TASI, 1999. Copyright FAQ. [online] http://ahds.ac.uk/bkgd/copyrightfaq.html (7 July 1999).

Albrecht, U., 1991. Factory tables as a source for a databank on the economic and social history of Flensburg of the 18th and 19th centuries. *History and computing,* 3(1), 36–44.

Anderson, M., Collins, B. and Stott, C., 1979. National Sample from the 1851 Census of Great Britain [computer file]. Colchester, Essex: The Data Archive [distributor]. SN: 1316.

Anderson, S., 1992. The future of the present – the ESRC Data Archive as a resource centre of the future. *History and computing,* 4(3), 191–96.

Bloothooft, G., 1995. Multi-source family reconstruction. *History and computing,* 7, 90–104.

Booth, C., 1892–1897. *Life and labour of the people in London.* 9 vols. 2nd ed. London: Macmillan & Co.

Bouchard, G. and Pouyez, C., 1980. Name variations and computerized record linkage. *Historical methods,* 13(2), 119–25.

Bradley, J., and Dupree, M., 1993. Interpreting datasets. The experience of third-party use of a machine readable 'source'. *History and computing,* 5(3), 169–79.

Burnard, L., 1989. Relational theory, SQL and historical practice. In: P. Denley, S. Fogelvik, and C. Harvey (eds.) *History and computing II.* Manchester: Manchester University Press, 63–71.

Burt, J. and Beaumont James, T., 1996. Source-orientated data processing. The triumph of the micro over the macro? *History and computing,* 8(3), 160–68.

CCTA, 1997. *PRINCE2, Project management for business.* London: The Stationary Office.

Champion, J., 1993. Relational databases and the Great Plague in London 1665. *History and computing,* 5 (1), 2–12.

Date, C.J., 1986. *Relational database. Selected writings.* New York: Addison-Wesley.

Date, C.J., 1989. *A guide to the SQL standard. A user's guide to the Standard Relational Language SQL.* Massachusetts: Addison-Wesley.

Date, C.J., 1994. *An introduction to database systems.* 6th ed. New York: Addison-Wesley.

Davies, H.R., 1992. Automated record linkage of census enumerators' books and registration data. Obstacles, challenges and solutions. *History and computing,* 4(1), 16–26.

Davis, V., 1990. Medieval English clergy database. *History and computing,* 2(2), 75–87.

Day, P.J., 1995. *Microsoft Project 4.0 for Windows and the Macintosh. Setting project management standards.* New York: Van Nostrand Reinhold.

Denley, P., 1994. Models, sources and users. Historical database design in the 1990s. *History and computing,* 6(1), 33–44.

Dupree, M., 1990. The medical profession in Scotland, 1911. The creation of a machine-readable database. In: E. Mawdsley *et al.* (eds.) *History and computing III. Historians, computers and data. Applications in research and teaching.* Manchester: Manchester University Press, 195–201.

Evans, R.J., 1997. *In defence of history.* London: Granta Books.

Feldman, M.S., 1995. *Strategies for interpreting qualitative data.* London: Sage.

Gahan, C. and Hannibal, M., 1997. *Doing qualitative research using QSR NUD*IST.* London: Sage.

Gervers, M.L.G. and McCulloch, M., 1990. The deeds database of mediaeval charters. Design and coding for the RDBMS Oracle 5. *History and computing,* 2(1), 1–11.

Green, E.M., 1989. Social structure and political behaviour in Westminster, 1748–1788. In: P. Denley, S. Fogelvik, and C. Harvey (eds.) *History and computing II*. Manchester: Manchester University Press, 239–42.

Green, E.M., 1990. The taxonomy of occupations in late eighteenth-century Westminster. In: P.J. Corfield and D. Keene (eds.) *Work in Towns, 850–1850*. Leicester: Leicester University Press, 164–81.

Greenstein, D I. (ed.), 1991. *Modelling historical data. Towards a standard for encoding and exchanging machine-readable texts*. St Katharinen: Max-Planck-Institut für Geschichte In Kommission bei Scripta Mercaturae Verlag.

Greenstein, D I., 1991. Standard, meta-standard. A framework for coding occupational data. *Historical social research/Historische sozialforschung*, 16(1), 3–22.

Greenstein, D. I., 1994. *A historians guide to computing*. Oxford: Oxford University Press.

Greenstein, D.I., 1989. A source-oriented approach to history and computing. The relational database. *Historical social research/Historische sozialforschung*, 14(3), 9–16.

GSU and FFHS, 1997. 1881 Census for England, Wales, Channel Islands and Isle of Man [computer file]. Colchester, Essex: The Data Archive [distributor]. SN: 3643.

GSU, 1988. *How transcribe the 1881 British census*. GSU: Salt Lake City.

Harvey, C. and Press, J., 1991. The business elite of Bristol. A case study in database design. *History and computing*, 3(1), 1–11.

Harvey, C. and Press, J., 1992. Relational data analysis. Value, concepts and methods. *History and computing*, 4(2), 98–109.

Harvey, C. and Press, J., 1993. Structured query language and historical computing. *History and computing*, 5(3), 154–69.

Harvey, C. and Press, J., 1996. *Databases in historical research. Theory, methods and applications*. London: Macmillan.

Harvey, C. and Taylor, P., 1987. Computer modelling and analysis of the individual aggregate capital stocks, cash flows and performance of British mining companies in Spain, 1851–1913. In: P. Denley and D. Hopkin (eds.) *History and computing*. Manchester: Manchester University Press, 115–20.

Harvey, C. and Taylor, P., 1988. The measurement and comparison of corporate productivity. Foreign and domestic firms in Spanish Mining in the late nineteenth century. *Histoire et mesure*, 3(1), 19–51.

Harvey, C., Green, E.M. and Corfield, P.J., 1996. Record linkage theory and practice. An experiment in the application of multiple pass linkage algorithms. *History and computing*, 8, 78–90.

Hatton, T.J. *et al.*, 1997. New Survey of London Life and Labour, 1929–1931 [computer file]. Colchester, Essex: The Data Archive [distributor]. SN: 3758.

Higgs, E., 1992. Machine-readable records, archives and historical memory. *History and computing*, 4(3), 183–190.

Howard, K. and Sharp, J.A., 1994. *The management of a student research project*. Aldershot: Gower.

Jaritz, G., 1991. The image as historical source or: Grabbing contexts. *Historical social research / Historische sozialforschung*. 16(4), 100–05.

Kelle, U. (ed.), 1995. *Computer-aided qualitative data analysis. Theory, methods and practice*. London: Sage.

King, S., 1992. Record linkage in a protoindustrial community. *History and computing*, 4(1), 27–33.

King, S., 1996. Historical demography, life-cycle reconstruction and family reconstruction. New perspectives. *History and computing*, 8, 62–78.

Mawdsley, E. and Munck, T., 1993. *Computing for historians. An introductory guide.* Manchester: Manchester University Press.

Miles, M.B. and Huberman, A.M., 1994. *Qualitative data analysis.* 2nd ed. London: Sage.

Millet, H., 1987. From sources to data. The construction of a prosopographical data-bank. In: P. Denley and D. Hopkin (eds.) *History and computing.* Manchester: Manchester University Press, 63–67.

Morris, R.J. and McCrum, A., 1995. Introduction. Wills, inventories and the computer. *History and computing,* 7, iv–xi.

Morris, R.J., 1990. Occupational coding. Principles and examples. *Historical social research/ Historische sozialforschung,* 15(1), 3–29.

Morrison, I.O., 1989. Data validation and dBase. *Computers and the history of art,* 10, 27–34.

Oldervoll, J., 1991. The machine-readable description of highly structured historical documents. Censuses and parish registers. In: D. Greenstein (ed.) *Modelling historical data. Towards a standard for encoding and exchanging machine-readable texts.* St Katharinen: Max-Planck-Institut für Geschichte In Kommission bei Scripta Mercaturae Verlag, 169–78.

Overton, M.A., 1995. Computer management system for probate inventories. *History and computing,* 7, 135–43.

Piotukh, N.V., 1996. The application of GIS techniques to Russian historical research. The Novorgev district used as a case study. *History and computing,* 8, 169–84.

Pöttler, B., 1990. Modelling historical data. Probate inventories as a source for the history of everyday life. In: F. Bocchi and P. Denley (eds.) *Storia & multimedia. Atti del settimo congresso internazionale – Association for History and Computing.* Bologna: Manchester University Press, 1990, 74–82.

Price, G. and Gray, A., 1994. Object oriented databases and their application to historical data. *History and computing,* 6(1), 44–52.

Robinson, P., 1993. *The digitisation of primary textual sources.* Oxford: Office for Humanities Communication.

Robinson, P., 1994. *The transcription of primary textual sources using SGML.* Oxford: Office for Humanities Communication.

Ruggles, S. and Menard, R.R., 1990. A public use sample of the 1880 U.S. Census of Population. *Historical methods.* 23(3), 104–15.

Scammell, L., 1997. Learning about relational databases. [online] http://seastorm.ncl.ac.uk/itti (7 July 1999).

Scammell, L., 1999. History, sailing and pages to support database advice. [online] http://seastorm.ncl.ac.uk/ (7 July 1999).

Schürer, K. and Diederiks, H., 1993. (eds.) *The use of occupations in historical analysis.* St Katharinen: Max-Planck-Institut für Geschichte In Kommission bei Scripta Mercaturae Verlag.

Schürer, K. and Oeppen, J., 1990. Calculating days of the week and some related problems with using calendars of the past. *History and computing,* 2(2), 107–18.

Schürer, K., 1990. The historical researcher and codes, master and slave or slave and master. In: E. Mawdsley *et al.* (eds.) *History and computing III. Historians, computers and data. Applications in research and teaching.* Manchester: Manchester University Press, 74–82.

Schürer, K., 1991. Standards or model solutions? The case of census-type documents. In: D. Greenstein (ed.) *Modelling historical data. Towards a standard for encoding and exchanging machine-readable texts.* St Katharinen: Max-Planck-Institut für Geschichte In Kommission bei Scripta Mercaturae Verlag, 205–23.

Schürer, K., 1996. Researching the population history of England. In: C. Harvey and J. Press

Databases in historical research. Theory, methods and applications. London: Macmillan, 253–256.

Silveira, L., Lopes, M. and Melo, C.Jd., 1995. Mapping Portuguese historical boundaries with a GIS. *Cahiers van de VGI*, 9, 245–53.

Southall, H. and Gregory, I., 1998. Historical GIS project home page. [online] http://www.geog.qmw.ac.uk/gbhgis (7 July 1999).

Spaeth, D.A., 1991. Court records and their structures. In: D. Greenstein (ed.) *Modelling historical data. Towards a standard for encoding and exchanging machine-readable texts.* St Katharinen: Max-Planck-Institut für Geschichte In Kommission bei Scripta Mercaturae Verlag, 129–45.

Thaller, M., 1980. Automation on Parnassus. CLIO – a databank orientated system for historians. *Historical Social Research/Historische Sozialforschung*, 15, 40–65.

Thaller, M., 1988a. A draft proposal for a standard format exchange program. In: J.P. Genet (ed.) *Standardisation et échange des bases de données historiques.* Paris: Éditions du Centre National de la Recherche Scientifique, 329–75.

Thaller, M., 1988b. Databases v. critical editions. *Historical social research/Historische sozialforschung*, 13(3), 129–39.

Thaller, M., 1989. The need for a theory of historical computing. In: P. Denley, S. Fogelvik, and C. Harvey, (eds.) *History and computing II.* Manchester: Manchester University Press, 2–11.

Thaller, M., 1991. The historical workstation project. *Historical social research/Historische sozialforschung*, 16(4), 51–61.

Thaller, M., 1993. *KLEIO. A database system.* St Katharinen: Max-Planck-Institut für Geschichte In Kommission bei Scripta Mercaturae Verlag.

Turner, J., 1989. Sex, age and the Labour vote in the 1920s. In: P. Denley, S. Fogelvik, and C. Harvey (eds.) *History and computing II.* Manchester: Manchester University Press, 243–54.

Wakelin, P. and Hussey, D., 1996. Investigating regional economies. The Gloucester Portbooks Database. In: C. Harvey and J. Press *Databases in historical research. Theory, methods and applications.* London: Macmillan, 14–21.

Wakelin, P., 1987. Comprehensive computerisation of a very large documentary source. The Portbooks Project at Wolverhampton Polytechnic. In: P. Denley and D. Hopkin (eds.) *History and computing.* Manchester: Manchester University Press, 109–15.

Weatherill, L. and Hemingway, V., 1994. *Using and designing databases for academic work. A practical guide.* Newcastle: Newcastle University.

Webb, C.C. and Hemingway V.W., 1995. Improving access. A proposal to create a database for the probate records at the Borthwick Institute. *History and computing*, 7, 152–56.

Welling, G.M., 1992. Intelligent large-scale historical direct-data-entry programming. In: J. Smets (ed.) *Histoire et informatique. Ve congrès "history and computing", 4–7 Septembre 1990 à Montpellier.* Association for History and Computing: Montpellier, 563–71.

Welling, G.M., 1993. A strategy for intelligent input programs for strucutred data. *History and computing*, 5(1), 35–41.

Woollard, M. and Denley, P. (eds.), 1996. *The sorcerers's apprentice. KLEIO case studies.* St Katharinen: Max-Planck-Institut für Geschichte In Kommission bei Scripta Mercaturae Verlag.

Wright, M., 1997. Part II. What do I do with it? [online] http:/dawww.essex.ac.uk/~melanie/iassist1.htm (7 July 1999).

Wrigley, E.A. and Schofield, R.S., 1973. Nominal record linkage by computer and the logic of family reconstitution. In: E.A. Wrigley (ed.) *Identifying people in the past.* Edward Arnold: London, 64–101.